Testosterone Replacement Therapy

The Truth about TRT: An Introductory Guide to Androgen Replacement Therapy and Hormone Replacement Therapy

presentation of the information is without contract or any type of guarantee assurance.

The trademarks that are used are without any consent, and the publication of the trademark is without permission or backing by the trademark owner. All trademarks and brands within this book are for clarifying purposes only and are owned by the owners themselves, not affiliated with this document.

Table of Contents

Introduction

You've probably heard about "TRT" at some point. Maybe you've heard about how it can rejuvenate middle aged men or give vitality to those who are depressed. So, what exactly is it?

This short and concise book provides introductory information on TRT treatments and how they may help people with hypogonadism and other needs. The content here isn't meant to be a form of medical advice, as this book is meant for informational purposes only. In this book we are aiming to look at this topic in an unbiased light. We are not promoting the use of TRT, per se, but we want to make sure that if someone is interested in this controversial topic, they can reach more informed conclusions.

We will discuss the history of TRT, the science behind it, and how it can affect one's body. Most practically, we will look at the pros and cons of this medical treatment and how it compares to other options.

We hope that you are able to learn a thing or two from   reading   this!

Chapter 1:

What is Testosterone Replacement Therapy?

Testosterone replacement therapy, also known as Androgen replacement therapy, is one of the most common types of hormone replacement therapies in our current society. During the process of this therapy, naturally recurring testosterone is replaced. The idea is to raise the low testosterone levels of an individual to what would be normal levels for them.

Androgen replacement therapy is often used for treating patients with hypogonadism, a medical condition resulting from the reduced biosynthesis of the sex hormones in both males and females. Simply put, this reduced testosterone level in men results in sexual dysfunction, reduced strength, a decrease in the body's muscle mass, a decrease in brain functioning and mood disturbance.

When testosterone levels have been restored to normal, or near normal, levels, patients almost always experience a relief from these aforementioned symptoms. Of course, there are risks involved and not all experts agree with this procedure, so we will briefly explore these points further in this book.

Available Treatments

There are various modes of hormonal treatment available to patients today. The earliest treatment modes included testosterone pellets that were implanted surgically on patients and testosterone esters that were injected. Nowadays, there are other treatment modalities that are less invasive than these options.

Today, there are patches and gels that are applied on a patient's skin to certain areas of the body, such as the male scrotum. The latest treatment method available to patients includes the administration of buccal tablets. Most noticeably, these new treatment options have piqued the interest of both doctors and patients to reconsider testosterone replacement therapy to treat hypogonadism.

Other Uses

In addition to hypogonadism, testosterone replacement therapy has become prevalent as a treatment option for a variety of conditions. One noticeable trend, in the last few decades, has been the utilization of TRT as a mode of treatment for men who want to delay the signs of aging. Note that men begin to experience a decline in their testosterone levels when they reach middle age, which is estimated to begin at the age of 35 to 40. At this time, men begin to experience all sorts of evident physical declines, such as fewer erections, a thinning of their skin, mental and physical fatigue, among other things.

The good news is that TRT can be used to treat all of these symptoms. Many who have undergone this therapy claim to they have regained their youthful strength and even obtained an increase in muscle mass. This type of hormone replacement therapy has also been credited with treating cancer patients who have lost their testicular function.

Note that, at the time of this publication, testosterone replacement therapy is quite controversial as a cancer treatment. There are medical experts who claim that this treatment method can help patients with prostate cancer and there are other experts who completely disagree. There are studies that demonstrate increased risks and there are studies that refute those said risks. Nothing is truly conclusive at this point.

Nevertheless, it has also been observed that symptoms like fatigue and low red blood cell counts have been improved with the help of TRT. There are currently studies underway that are trying to discover if TRT can be used to treat additional medical conditions, such as chronic heart failure, dementia, diabetes mellitus, osteoporosis, and erectile dysfunction. However, because hormone replacement therapy is relatively understudied at this point in time, there is little data and even less evidence to work with.

Chapter 2:

The History of TRT Treatment

While the development of TRT can be credited to the prevalence of hypogonadism in the medical field, this form of treatment is based on a premise that is much older - organotherapy.

Simply put, the idea behind organotherapy is to treat an illness with a thing that is like unto it. This concept of treatment leads us all the way back to the days of antiquity. You can even say that testosterone replacement therapy can trace its very foundation from folklore medicine.

Verification by Medical Research

Even though the root of the premise behind TRT treatment goes back to folklore, no one can readily dismiss its merits simply because of such grounds. In fact, the very foundation of testosterone replacement is based on three different pieces of foundational research, namely the research conducted by Berthauld (1849), the self-experimentation by Brown-Sequard (1189), and Myers and Heller's article published in JAMA (1944).

Charles-Edouard Brown-Sequard was a physician and a physiologist. He presented the results of his experiments in 1889 before the Society de Biologie of Paris. In his presentation, he explained that he experimented on himself – which made this one of the most curious cases of self-experimentation in history. Brown-Sequard used testicular extracts taken from dogs, as well as guinea pigs, and injected them into himself.

He described the effects of such experiments in very emotional and descriptive words. He mentions regaining his youthful strength, a marked improvement in his mental faculties, and other related benefits. In essence, his claims sounded very much like the ones one would hear from people who rave about TRT treatments and its health benefits in our current age.

Of course, to verify his claims, other scientists of the time took the 72-year-old man's extract to find traces of androgen. Unfortunately, they didn't find any, so it was concluded that whatever rejuvenation Brown-Sequard gained was nothing more than a mere placebo effect.

However, the ruckus that Brown-Sequard created drew a lot of interest from the public. This inevitably made other researchers and scientists look into the possibility of testosterone supplementation. It also inspired Leopold Ruzicka and Adolf Butenandt to conduct the research and experiments that would eventually synthesize testosterone. Their work actually won them a Nobel Prize in 1939.

However, even before Brown-Sequard inspired others to dig deeper into the less understood world of the male hormone, Professor Arnold A. Berthold had already recorded his observations in 1849. He was the curator of a local zoo at the time and he conducted related experiments on roosters.

In his experiments, Berthold learned that certain body parts were actually androgen dependent. He observed that when he castrated a rooster, its comb size and shape eventually receded and its interests in mating with hens disappeared. He concluded that the testes affected the blood of an organism, and the blood of the organism that was castrated then acts on the body, thus producing the effects he observed.

Even more interesting was what came next. Berthold observed that transplanting the removed testes back to the rooster could reverse the symptoms. The rooster's comb regained its original appearance. The rooster's interest in hens, and other masculine-associated behaviors, such as crowing, also returned to normal. This was the first time that the hormone called "testosterone" was discovered. Some historians even believe that this marked the beginning of endocrinology.

The last formative bit of science, which served as one of the backbones of modern TRT therapies, was the paper produced by Gordon Myers and Carl Heller. The paper submitted by these two Detroit internists fundamentally showed that many of the symptoms that men experience as they age could be attributed to hypogonadism.

The symptoms that they referred to included loss of sexual vigor, fatigue, memory impairment, and depression. Now, even though Heller and Myers didn't have the technology to actually measure serum testosterone levels in men in their day-to-day lives, they devised methods to diagnose their patients.

Their methods were practical in a way and quite ingenious in another, given the limits of the technology at the time. First off, they used testicular biopsies to diagnose the male climacteric. They also used a bioassay to test for levels of urinary gonadotropin. It was already established at the time that castrated men had increased gonadotropin levels. Also, it had been established scientifically that normal, healthy men, and even men with psychogenic impotence, still had normal levels of gonadotropin.

However, just like in Berthold's case, the last part of their experiment was one that truly piqued the curiosity of the public. They administered testosterone propionate to patients with low gonadotropin levels, and the results were astounding. Not only did their patients regain normal gonadotropin levels but also the symptoms that these same patients experienced were also reduced.

Soon after, some entrepreneurs tried to produce testosterone tablets for consumption. However, it was soon discovered that the testosterone was not integrating with the body as desired, and instead it was being eliminated after passing through the liver. So, then came the modality of implanting the tablets subcutaneously (i.e. under the skin). Note that this was one of the early treatment modes that were available, other than inoculation.

TRT Treatments to Date

The few decades from the 1950's to the 1970's marked very little improvement in the development of testosterone preparations for the treatment of hypogonadism. Even though the market called for it, the pharmaceutical industry never responded to the demand.

Instead, it focused on the production of androgens that were synthesized for muscle growth because that's where the money was. Unfortunately, most of these products actually disappeared when legislation was passed that demanded for proof of their efficacy.

Today, there is still a lot of debate regarding testosterone replacement therapy, specifically as a treatment for hypogonadism. There are pros and cons and, of course, people claim that there is evidence on both sides of this issue.

Chapter 3:

The Science Behind TRT Treatments

Testosterone is a hormone that is present in both men and women. Because its main purpose is to promote the growth and development of masculine-associated tissues, it is understandable why men produce more of this hormone than women. In order to understand the science behind TRT, one must understand how the body naturally produces this hormone.

The Road to Testosterone Production

The human body undergoes a long and complex process in order to produce testosterone. The entire process begins at the base of the brain - the hypothalamus. The hypothalamus secretes a substance called gonadotropin-releasing hormone, which we will refer to as GnRH for short. GnRH is then released into the pituitary gland.

This hormone causes the pituitary gland to produce two other hormones: luteinizing hormone (LH) and follicle-stimulating hormone (FSH). These two hormones are collectively referred to as gonadotropins. Of these two hormones, luteinizing hormone is the most important in this context because it is the one that travels via the blood stream and all the way to the testes.

 LH eventually reaches the testes, and when it does, it stimulates activity among the Leydig cells. It is at this point where the synthesis, or production, of testosterone begins. Simply put, the body converts cholesterol into testosterone.

An increase at any point during this process of the chain of chemicals that triggers the production of testosterone can speed up its production in the body. The entire production process continues until the male hormonal levels in the body become too high. Going back to the process, it can be easy to see that luteinizing hormone is the key hormone that can be used to increase the natural production of testosterone in the body.

Note that testosterone is not released as it is in the blood stream. It requires a carrier compound called SHBG, also referred to as sex hormone binding globulin. This carrier compound is produced in the liver and regulates the amount of testosterone in the blood. If the levels of SHBG rise, then the testosterone levels in the blood rise as well. If the SHBG levels fall, then testosterone levels fall as well.

A Very Complex Production Process

As you can see, there are several factors in a complex chain of events that can affect the levels of testosterone in the body. This means that there could be any number of factors along the way that can affect the rise and fall of testosterone levels or its production. When men get to the age of 35, it is estimated that the total testosterone production in their bodies has already gone down by as much as 50 percent of what was once its peak production level.

This reduced level of production brings about certain symptoms, such as mood swings, depression, loss of concentration, and an eventual loss of energy. When the amount of testosterone in the blood stream goes down, it doesn't necessarily mean that a man's reproductive system will stop working as well. Nevertheless, some people believe that this huge reduction in male hormonal levels in the blood can lead to certain episodes of impotence, which is debatable at this point in time.

Testosterone Replacement Therapy Approaches

There are several approaches to TRT treatment. Medical professionals will usually recommend bypassing the long and arduous track that the body goes through. Doing so helps avoid affecting the complex chemical processes described earlier. One of the most commonly recommended treatment methods is via steroid injections, and the treatments can be scheduled either on a weekly or bi-weekly basis.

Doctors usually prescribe an androgen hormone that is water based. Note that this is a very effective process. The only drawback is that it is relatively expensive compared to other options on the market. A long-term downside is that the body may become dependent on these synthetic testosterone injections and the body's entire mechanism for naturally producing testosterone can get atrophied, so the natural male hormonal production process of the body eventually shuts down.

Of course, bypassing the androgen production system is only one of several approaches to testosterone replacement therapy. In fact, there are actually more ways to enhance natural testosterone production than methods of bypassing it altogether. The main idea of course is to influence the body by providing it with all the things it needs to produce testosterone. Some medical experts believe that this is definitely the better alternative, especially for men who still have many decades of life to live.

For instance, certain medications are designed to influence the body's production of LH. Nevertheless, taking these medications will still require other contributory activities, such as a programmed workout and a high protein diet. Some of these medications may also require stress reduction and sufficient amounts of sleep. The idea, of course, is to create an environment that is naturally conducive to the production of androgens.

Chapter 4:

Effects of Testosterone Replacement Therapy

Testosterone replacement therapy tries to reverse the conditions brought about by low levels of androgens in the body. Note that the amount or level of male hormones that must be restored will differ from one patient to the other. The age of a patient also becomes an important factor, so the restoration of testosterone levels should be done in degrees.

Effects of TRT Treatments

Are there any effects, immediate or otherwise, when people undergo testosterone replacement therapy? The short answer is yes. Some people may stir up controversy by answering in the affirmative, yet the unequivocal answer to that simple question is yes - there are positive effects when people undergo this type of hormone replacement therapy.

Improvement in Bone Mineral Density

For instance, in one study that was conducted by Snyder and company in 1999, it was found that a patient's bone mineral density improved after supplementing with testosterone. It was found effective for patients that had baseline testosterone levels of 3 ng/ml.

Improvement in Energy Levels and Mood

In a study published by Cambridge University Press in 2004, it was found that after undergoing TRT treatment, some male patients experienced mood improvements and an increase in energy levels. In turn, these changes brought about a radical improvement in these men's overall well being.

Improvement from Anemic Conditions

Some patients showed improvement from anemic conditions, which is a symptom of hypogonadism. Researchers like Behre, Daniell, Mittan, Felsenberg, and Francis all agree in their various publications that hypogonadism is the single most important cause of osteoporosis in men today. Their studies were published from 1993 to 2002. They point out that a decrease in the testosterone levels in men brings about bone loss in various areas of a man's skeletal system, which includes the hip, femoral neck, and lumbar spine.

Used as Marker for Treatment Efficacy

In the studies conducted by Behre (published in 1997) and by Zitzman (published in 2002), it was shown that testosterone replacement greatly benefitted hypogonadal men that had reduced bone mass density. The improvements were observed over several years – meaning that there is no such thing as an instant treatment. This also translates to the fact that TRT treatment is not some sort of magic pill that can make a man's troubles go away in a week.

Potential Effects on Cardiovascular System

There are also potential effects of testosterone replacement therapy on the cardiovascular system. However, this particular effect is a bit controversial. In March of 2015, the United States Food and Drug Administration (FDA) made an announcement regarding a possible increased risk for people undergoing TRT treatments who have cardiovascular health issues.

Of course, some people disagreed with the decision made by the FDA committee. The concern over the effects of testosterone on cardiovascular health are based on the fact that men are more prone to heart disease and other related conditions in comparison to women, and such fears and concerns were not unfounded.

Chapter 5:

Pros and Cons of TRT Treatments

Since 1993, there has been an upsurge in the sales of TRT related prescription medication. This steady record in sales is due in part to effective marketing. However, one can't give advertisers all of the credit. Any effort on their part wouldn't mean anything in the long run if the actual medications they were selling didn't produce any real results. The bottom line is that people still continue to buy TRT treatment products after all these years simply because they work as advertised.

While the effects of TRT were laid out in the previous chapter, let's now take a look a look at the pros and cons.

Reviewing the Pros

Note that there is no 100% guarantee that you will also experience exactly the same gains if you undergo a similar hormone replacement therapy. Please be advised that you should seek medical advice to determine whether this treatment will be necessary in order to obtain your desired benefits.

Improving Erectile Dysfunction

Hemmingsen and Lyngdorf (Int J Impot Res. 2004) have pointed out that as men age there is a marked increase in the prevalence of erectile dysfunction. It was found that older men required more testosterone in their system in order to attain proper erectile function and a healthy libido.

These patients are often candidates for treatment using TRT. Controlled clinical trials show that testosterone replacement therapy produces positive health related benefits. It has also been shown to help with the frequency of erections during sleep.

Improved Bone Density

Hypogonadism has also been related to other dysfunctions, which include a lowered bone mass. Men who experience osteopenia and osteoporosis have a high probability of being androgen deficient as well. It has been found that osteoporosis is more prevalent in men with lower than normal androgen levels.

Studies also show that the increase (or decrease) of testosterone levels in men has a role to play in the body's bone mineral density. However, do take note that testosterone replacement will not make the body reach exactly the same normal adult bone mass.

It's important that the amount of testosterone substituted is high enough to achieve a near normal bone mineral density. Remember that TRT is only a treatment and not a miracle cure, which it is sometimes advertised as by companies.

Improved Body Composition

As people grow older, their body composition also changes. These changes are quite significant and they affect a person's physical stature and overall well-being. The body undergoes a redistribution of fat mass and there is also a decrease in the body's fat-free mass. Inevitably, this also means a reduction in a person's strength levels.

Some of these changes can eventually lead to an increase in morbidity or at least may impose certain physical limitations on people when they grow older.

Many studies have shown that TRT can bring about an increase in muscle mass, an increase in strength, and improve the body's composition as a whole. Some studies have shown that patients have gained more lean body mass and significant decreased their body's fat mass. An increase in arm circumference was also observed, along with improved grip strength in older men.

Even though these studies are currently still few, it can already be observed that a significant increase in lower body strength is observable. Some cross sectional studies have shown that there is a possible correlation between muscle strength and testosterone levels in older men. Admittedly, more studies need to be executed to confirm these results to a point of being undeniable.

Improved Mood

Hypogonadal men usually exhibit many of the symptoms mentioned here in this book, such as irritability, fatigue, dysphoria, and loss of libido. It should be noted that these symptoms usually overlap with depression in men.

One study shows that both obese and underweight men can get relief from depression symptoms with the help of TRT treatment. However, there isn't always a linear correlation between a man's mood and the level of androgens. It appears that the changes in mood, and ultimately depression, in men are independent of weight and age.

There are studies that show that hypogonadal men improve from depression symptoms, which means testosterone replacement can be a good anti-depressant option. However, the subjects of these studies were hypogonadal men with Major Depressive Disorder (MDD). Another study compared the effects of placebo with that of TRT treatments (specifically the use of testosterone gel), and the group that was administered testosterone gel showed a greater improvement in testosterone levels.

Cognitive Function

One hypothesis in regards to cognitive function is that as the bioavailable testosterone decreases in a man's body, that man's cognitive function and capability also decreases. It is said that as a man grows older, his verbal and visual memory also decreases.

To support this hypothesis, a study was conducted involving Alzheimer's patients. The sample also included age-matched controls. It was found that these patients had a lower ratio of SHBG to total testosterone.

There were also other tests and studies conducted that concerned the relationship of testosterone levels with age related cognitive functions. From what little clinical trials are currently available, it can be assumed that there are at least a few cognitive deficits that can be reversed using TRT treatments. However, the duration and amount of recovery is still in question.

Reviewing the Cons

Bone Mineral Density

It has been pointed out that TRT treatments may help improve bone mineral density. However, do take note that studies also show that the results are less promising for older men. Yes, controlled clinical trials have shown improvement in bone density in the hips and such improvements have reduced the patient's risk for fractures. However, there are cases when such improvements are not significant enough to improve a patient's quality of life, and note that this downside mainly concerns aging men.

Not So Impressive Bodily Improvement

There are studies and cases where the improvement in lean body mass isn't impressive or significant, even after a bi-weekly administration of testosterone. At most, the improvements in bodily composition can be said to be modest in most men. The same can be said of the reduction in fat mass.

However, it is important to note that this is heavily based on a man's natural body composition throughout his life. Genetics play a large role in this aspect of TRT treatment. Men who are naturally muscular and have a hard time putting on body fat will usually obtain different results than those who were the opposite all their lives. Nonetheless, improvements in body composition are helpful, even if they don't turn you into the Hulk.

Mood Improvement

Although there are case studies in which patients did experience an improvement from depressive symptoms, not every controlled study exhibited the same result. There have been placebo-controlled studies that also compared results with that of TRT treatments and both groups fundamentally showed the same results.

This means that there is a possibility that there is no distinguishable improvement when you compare the effects of placebo and TRT treatments. The Massachusetts Male Aging Study also confirmed that, at least in their trials, there was no correlation between mood improvements (including relief from depressive symptoms) and the rise and fall of testosterone levels.

Some Possible Side Effects

While the severity and occurrence of these side effects differ from person to person, we've provided a list of possible side effects that can range from nonexistent to bothersome. To avoid or decrease the chance of these side effects, check your health markers with your doctor before starting any TRT treatment protocol.

Stimulated growth of existing prostate cancer

Deep vein thrombosis

Sleep apnea

Breast enlargement

Testicle shrinkage

Balancing the Risks and Benefits

As with any treatment, there are benefits and risks that one must balance during their decision-making process. Paracelsus once said that the dosage alone could dictate whether something can be considered a remedy or a poison. In this case, it means that you must work with your doctor to find that balance to make a TRT treatment work effectively for you.

Chapter 6:

TRT Treatments Compared to Alternatives

Note that there are alternatives to testosterone replacement therapy currently on the market and it is in your best interest to consider the range of these treatments. Another fact that everyone must consider is that some of the symptoms of hypogonadism are similar to other medical conditions, so further medical evaluation should be undergone before assuming that what you are experiencing is hypogonadism.

Nutrients That Can Boost Testosterone Levels

Certain nutrients, such as zinc and vitamin D, can help boost testosterone levels. People with low testosterone levels usually have low levels of these nutrients as well. Foods that are rich in zinc include raw eggs, beans, yogurt, fish, meat, and oysters. You can increase your vitamin D intake by consuming it in supplement form (tablet) or by gaining healthy sun exposure.

Exercise and Weight Loss

Another alternative to TRT treatment is managing one's weight and engaging in regular exercise routines. This can help the body increase testosterone levels naturally. Along with active meditation sessions, exercise will help to reduce your stress levels, which in turn will raise the natural state of testosterone within your body.

Alternative Medication

There are certain medications that can also help supplement low testosterone levels. Examples of which include clomiphene, aromatase inhibitors, and chorionic gonadotropin. Note that these medications work on the body's natural testosterone processes instead of directly supplementing the body's ready supply.

These alternative methods do not always provide immediate results. So, this means that you will have to wait for the benefits to become evident. Also, just like TRT, there is still a lot of research that needs to be done in regards to these treatment methods.

Chapter 7:

The Future of Testosterone Replacement

There is still a lot of ground that needs to be covered in the field of testosterone replacement therapy. However, many experts in the field believe that things are looking bright and that current research is on track. There are many facets that should be addressed, but the good news is that there is a growing body of professionals who are rallying behind this therapy, providing their support and doing the relevant research.

Testosterone Replacement Therapy and Cardio Health

One of the most important issues raised against testosterone replacement therapy are the effects on the cardiovascular health of patients. As mentioned earlier, this is basically the reason why the United States FDA has instructed that every single testosterone product in the market today should add a warning line to their product labels. That new line on the label basically warns consumers that the contents may increase the possible risk of cardiovascular diseases.

However, Dr. Abraham Morgentaler of Harvard believes that new studies on this issue will come along in the next five years. He says that there are studies that test whether testosterone is bad for the heart and they are all negative. In these studies, Dr. Morgentaler further states that it shows that there may actually be benefits instead of increased risk.

Morgentaler also believes that we will one day, in the near future, learn all the benefits of having normal testosterone levels versus having low testosterone levels later in life. He admits that there is currently a growing body of data that supports this belief. Morgentaler summarizes that current data supports the fact that men with low testosterone levels tend to die earlier than men with normal testosterone levels.

One such study that may be used for evidence for this is the one conducted by the Veterans Association, which was published in 2008. The study concludes that increased mortality rate in men was directly associated with a decrease in testosterone levels. Morgentaler believes that there will be studies that will be conducted in the future to find out the interrelationship between these facts.

Other experts are also looking into testosterone replacement therapy as a possible treatment for prostate cancer. Some believe that this is another field where a lot of studies will be conducted. It is expected that there will be future studies and trials that will determine plausibility of dietary manipulation as a mode for this therapy.

Conclusion

Thank you for reading this! We hope this short, concise book was able to teach you a thing or two about the intriguing TRT treatment.

Now that you understand the important factors regarding TRT, you can decide if you want to try it, or if you can inform your friends who ask you about it. Plus, a little addition to your knowledge doesn't hurt, right? Our world is becoming increasingly interested in the use of exogenous hormones, whether it be for sex changes, physical transformations, or as medical assistance to those who need it.

If you've learned anything from this book, please take the time to share your thoughts by sending me a personal message, or even posting a review on Amazon. It would be greatly appreciated and I try my best to get back to every message!

Thank you and good luck in your journey!

www.ingramcontent.com/pod-product-compliance
Lightning Source LLC
Chambersburg PA
CBHW070326290526
45791CB00003B/1277